THE BELOVED DISCIPLE:
WITNESS AGAINST ANTI-SEMITISM

THE BELOVED DISCIPLE: WITNESS AGAINST ANTI-SEMITISM

Philip S Kaufman OSB

The Liturgical Press

Collegeville, Minnesota

Library of Congress Cataloging-in-Publication Data

Kaufman, Philip S., 1911–
    The Beloved Disciple : witness against anti-Semitism / Philip S.
Kaufman.
        p.   cm.
    ISBN 0-8146-2067-1
    1. Bible. N.T. John—Criticism, interpretation, etc.
2. Christianity and antisemitism. 3. Beloved Disciple. I. Title.
BS2615.6.J44K38 1991   91-12951
261.2′6—dc20   CIP

To
the members
of my adult education classes
with whom I learned to see things new!

Contents

Introduction

I was born in 1911 into a Reform Jewish family in Vicksburg, Mississippi, a small southern town that was still fighting the Civil War. In 1917 we lived on Baum Street, a short street of only a block and a half where there were four other Jewish families, including our rabbi, Dr Sol Kory. With the flu epidemic and America's entrance into World War I, it was not a good year. Suddenly my good friend, Hans, disappeared. My grandmother, Sarah Feld, explained to me that his father was an officer in the German army. It was heavy stuff for a six-year old.

Since kindergarten had not yet been introduced in Vicksburg, 1917 was my first year at Speed Street School. I came home one day troubled that John Lee, who lived around the corner, was related to General Robert E. Lee and I wasn't related to anyone important. Grandmother came to the rescue and explained that I was descended from King David and that there had been someone named David in each generation of our family as far back as anyone could remember.

I was the only Jewish boy in the first grade. I don't think grandmother solved the problem when I was chased home from school because I was a Christ-killer. I didn't even know who Christ was and I was sure that I had never killed anyone.

I don't remember discussions of anti-Semitism in our home. It was quite by accident that I overheard one of my parents repeat a conversation between the rabbi and Mrs Mackey, a devout Methodist who lived across the street. "Dr Kory," she had said, "you are the source of great sorrow for me." "Why, Mrs Mackey, what have I done?" he asked. "Oh! It isn't anything you have done. You are one of the most wonderful men I have ever known. It grieves me so, that you're going to suffer in hell for all eternity."

There was, however, great emphasis as I grew up that as a Jew I would have to study and work harder to be treated as well as my Christian friends.

After my family moved to New York in 1934 and I began to work at B. Altman's, the well-known department store, I came under the influence of a devout, proselytizing Roman Catholic executive named Dan Sullivan who tricked me into attending Mass. Under his influence I had a conversion experience that pointed me toward the Benedictines. I ended up at St Anselm's rectory in the Bronx under the tutelage of Fr Gerald McMahon, a monk of St John's Abbey in Collegeville, Minnesota.

At the time I was a professed agnostic with anti-Semitic leanings. Fr Gerald informed me that we would first have to decide if I was going to become a Catholic; then we would decide if I was to become a Benedictine. He also convinced me that I must not deny my Jewish roots and that I should always remain proud of my Jewish heritage. So for over fifty years I have considered myself a Christian Jew.

I do not recall any anti-Semitic preaching or teaching in those early years. Only after I had been baptized in 1938 and gone to St John's Abbey the following year did I encounter one isolated, unofficial situation. As we learned of Hitler's persecution of the Jews in the 1940s, I discussed

Introduction

10

this with my novice master and scripture professor, Fr Basil Stegmann. His explanation was very simple. What was happening to the Jews in Germany was the result of the curse their ancestors had called down upon them when they had cried out before Pilate, "His blood be upon us and upon our children" (Mt 27:25).

Anyone who studied scripture in a Roman Catholic seminary in the early forties should be aware not just of the inadequacy of what was learned, but also of much that was inaccurate in bible studies before the liberating, 1943 encyclical of Pius XII, *Divino Afflante Spiritu*. Since the best way to learn is to teach, I decided to update my knowledge of scripture by adding a series on "Jesus in the Church's Gospels" to my courses in adult education. The course was eventually narrowed down to five sessions, often taught in Lent, entitled "The Passion and Death of Our Lord in the Four Gospels."

Each student in the class had a copy of the four gospel accounts in parallel. We began with the arrest of Jesus in Mark, widely thought to be the first Gospel to have been written. Then we moved to the Gospels of Matthew and Luke whose writers are assumed to have had the Gospel of Mark before them when they wrote, and asked why they had changed the text of Mark. Last we went to John, probably written independently of the other three. So step by step we worked our way through the four Gospels down to the burial.

In the course of this teaching/learning experience I made a fascinating discovery: there are two significantly different accounts of the passion in the

Gospels. The very similar accounts in Mark and Matthew place the major responsibility on the Jews and emphasize the role of Jewish leaders and people; the account in John suggests the likelihood of collusion between the Roman procurator Pontius Pilate and Caiaphas, the Jewish high priest, and gives no indication of participation by the people. Luke's account is usually close to that in John.

It is widely agreed that teaching and preaching based on the Gospels contributed to the "teaching of contempt" and through it to two millennia of anti-Semitism. It became clear in my teaching/learning experience that past teaching and preaching on the passion had been based almost exclusively on Matthew and Mark and that John had been almost completely ignored. It therefore became important to me to know which of the two accounts is historically more credible. I reached the conclusion that when the Gospels disagree, we should take the evidence of John seriously.

I published the results of this study experience in an essay in *Worship*.[1] Only after I began the task of developing the essay further did I read Bishop John A. T. Robinson's *Redating the New Testament*[2] and *The Priority of John*.[3] Many scholars who reject Robinson's conclusion that the Gospel of John was written by the Beloved Disciple, traditionally identified as John the son of Zebedee, acknowledge that Robinson has often discovered elements of historical significance in that Gospel. Although I also do not accept everything in Robinson, my reading of him has led to changes in my original essay that reinforce my thesis.

Anyone who has read widely in biblical studies is

Introduction

aware of the high level of disagreement among biblical scholars. On the issues that will arise in this study, competent scholars can usually be quoted on either side. For almost two thousand years, an account of the passion, based almost exclusively on Mark and Matthew, has been taught and preached in the Christian churches, contributing to centuries of virulent anti-Judaism. By taking advantage of our new awareness of the historical value of John's Gospel, I propose to construct, from among the varying opinions of competent scholars, a highly plausible version of the passion that is solidly based on the minimally anti-Semitic account of the Beloved Disciple. Of him the Gospel testifies, "This is the disciple who is bearing witness to these things, and who has written these things; and we know that his testimony is true" (Jn 21:24).

Linda Mealey has again proved herself to be a superb editor. The endnotes give only slight evidence of the help I have received from Gerard S. Sloyan. Others who have helped especially are Knute Anderson OSB; Frank Kacmarcik OBL.SB; Michael Fortier, my student research assistant; and the always cooperative staffs of Academic Computing, especially Anthony Heid, and the Alcuin Library of St John's University. I alone, however, am responsible for what I have written.

Introduction

"The Teaching of Contempt"[4]

Contrary to those writers who consider
contemporary anti-Semitism a completely modern
phenomenon, or claim that it derives from early
pagan anti-Semitism rather than from Christian
sources, it is now widely recognized that biblical
accounts of the passion were an important element
in the centuries of anti-Semitism in Christian
Europe that culminated in the Holocaust.[5]

Shifting of blame on to the Jews begins already in
Paul's First Letter to the Thessalonians, with its
reference to "the Jews, who killed both the Lord
Jesus and the prophets" (2:14-15). It continues in
the speeches in Acts, with Peter's first sermon on
Pentecost, "men of Israel . . . this Jesus
. . . you crucified and killed by the hands of
lawless men" (2:22-23, 36; also 3:13-15 and 4:10);
with Stephen, "the Righteous One, whom you have
now betrayed and murdered" (7:52); and with Paul
in the synagogue in Antioch in Pisidia, "For those
who live in Jerusalem and their rulers . . . asked
Pilate to have him killed" (13:27-28).

As early as the third century, Tertullian
(c 160-230) wrote of the transmission of guilt to
later generations in his treatise *On Prayer*:
"Although Israel may wash all its limbs daily,
nevertheless it is never clean. Certainly its hands
are always unclean, crusted over forever with the
blood of the prophets and of the Lord himself; and
therefore those hereditarily guilty due to the
conscience of their ancestors, do not even dare to
raise their hands to the Lord."[6]

Moreover, according to Tertullian, it is primarily
Matthew's report that "all the people cried, 'His

The Teaching of Contempt

14

blood be upon us and upon our children'" that has caused all Jews through the centuries to be held responsible for the crucifixion. As Tertullian wrote, "And so the whole synagogue of the sons of Israel killed him saying to Pilate, when he wished to release him: 'Let the blood of this man be upon us and upon our children.'"[7]

Origen (c 185-245), in a device used over and over again by subsequent writers, quoted a passage from the prophet Isaiah to emphasize Jewish blood guilt through all generations. He wrote that while Pilate "washed himself; they, however, not only did not wish to cleanse themselves of the blood of Christ, but even took it upon themselves saying: 'His blood be upon us and upon our children.' Because of this, they are not only guilty of the blood of the prophets, but filling the measure of their fathers, they are guilty of the blood of Christ, that they might hear God saying to them: 'When you shall have extended your hands to me, I shall turn my eyes from you; your hands are full of blood' (Is 1:15). For that reason, the blood of Jesus is not only on those who lived then, but indeed upon all the generations of Jews following after until the end. Therefore even now their home has been forsaken and deserted by them."[8]

In the fourth century, Eusebius, the early church historian, having quoted the passage from Isaiah, wrote, "This blood of so long ago deprives them of happiness; this blood has declared them the outcasts of the world."[9] St Hilary of Poitiers compared the Jews to Cain who killed his innocent brother, "It is the blood of all the just that their whole flesh and all their generations take upon

The Teaching of Contempt

themselves while they themselves cry out, 'His blood be upon us and upon our children.'"[10] And St Jerome, using Isaiah, wrote, "This curse continues today upon the Jews, and the blood of the Lord is not taken away from them . . . this last inheritance to their children."[11]

In his sermons *Adversus Judaeos* (387), St John Chrysostom used the most vitriolic devices of the rhetoricians of his day in an effort to stop the many Christians in Antioch and other cities of the east from worshiping with their Jewish neighbors on the high holidays.[12] To the Jews, not present of course, with whom his wayward Christians were fasting and praying, Chrysostom proclaimed: "You did slay Christ, you did lift violent hands against the Master, you did spill his precious blood. This is why you have no chance of atonement, excuse, or defense."[13] Chrysostom's sermons, the most popular of his writings, made an important contribution to the evil litany that continued through the centuries. They were incorporated into the Byzantine liturgy of Holy Week and translated into Russian in the eleventh century when Jewish homes were plundered and the first pogrom in Russian history took place under Prince Vladimir in the grand duchy of Kiev.[14]

In the sixteenth century, Luther wrote, "I am of the opinion that this is a curse which is still bearing down hard on them."[15] His "Tract Concerning the Jews and their Lies" (1543) contains his notorious recommendation "to set fire to their synagogues or schools and to bury and cover with dirt whatever will not burn . . . that their homes be razed and destroyed . . . that all their prayer books

The Teaching of Contempt

16

and Talmudic writings, in which such idolatry, lies, cursing, and blasphemy are taught, be taken from them . . . that their rabbis be forbidden to teach henceforth on pain of loss of life and limb."[16]

As recently as the middle of the nineteenth century, in an influential work translated into several languages and republished in English in 1949, four years after the discovery of the Nazi gas chambers, the French Benedictine Abbot Prosper Guéranger wrote in *The Liturgical Year: Passiontide and Holy Week*, "Like the tiger that grows fiercer as he sees blood, so is Israel at the sight of Jesus after His scourging 'Crucify Him! Crucify Him!'. . . . They answer him [Pilate] with this terrible self-imprecation: 'His Blood be upon us and upon our children!' The mark of parricide here fastens on this ungrateful and sacrilegious people; Cain-like, they shall wander as fugitives upon the earth. Eighteen hundred years have passed since then: slavery, misery, and contempt have been their portion, but the mark is still upon them."[17]

The passage from Matthew, interpreted as placing responsibility on all subsequent generations of Jews, became so deeply ingrained in the mentality of Christian writers and preachers through the centuries that it did not even have to be expressed, but was always understood. The promoters of the passion play in Oberammergau were recently persuaded to dress the actors who took the parts of Jesus and the apostles as Jews, but were unwilling to give up the cry, "His blood be upon us and our children."

The song "Alas for you," in Stephen Schwartz'
new lyrics for "Godspell," ends,

> Blind guides! Blind fools!
> The blood you've spilt
> On you will fall
> This nation, this generation
> Shall bear the guilt
> Of it all!
>
> Alas, alas, alas
> Blind fools!

The lyrics of the popular rock opera, *Jesus Christ
Superstar*, do not have the passage from Matthew
27:25, but keep repeating the cry of the mob
"Crucify him."

Two Different Accounts

What has not been widely noticed is that the Gospels do not yield a simple unified account of who was originally responsible for the crucifixion. A careful comparison reveals that the account in John is significantly different from that in Mark and Matthew. Moreover, when there is disagreement among the Synoptics in the passion narrative, Luke is usually closer to John than to Mark and Matthew. While many scholars are convinced that Luke had Mark before him when he wrote his Gospel, for the passion he seems also to have used a primitive written source that is closer to the events and more historically accurate than Mark.[18]

From early years in the church down to our own day, an account of the passion based almost entirely on Mark and Matthew has been used to support widespread Christian teaching that the Jewish people and authorities were fully responsible for Jesus' arrest, trials and sentencing. The Romans were perceived to be little more than executioners. While for centuries the account of the passion in John, which is minimally a source of the virulent anti-Semitic propaganda in Christian Europe, has been virtually ignored.

The quite different account of the passion in John can provide much needed correction on several critical points. First, it suggests the possibility of greater involvement of the Romans than do the Synoptics. Moreover, John has no account of a night trial before the Jewish great council that according to Mark and Matthew condemned Jesus to death for blasphemy. Luke has only a morning hearing before the council but without a charge of blasphemy or a verdict.[19] John, as opposed to the Synoptics, gives no evidence of the involvement of the people either in the arrest of Jesus or in his trial before Pilate. In John only some of the Jerusalem officials and Temple guards cry out to Pilate "Crucify him" (19:6), and no one is reported to have mocked Jesus as he hung upon the cross.

On the other hand, in an issue we will explore later, it must be conceded that a consistent, though often inaccurate translation of John's *hoi Ioudaioi* as "the Jews," has done plenty of mischief.

Two Different Accounts

20

The Credibility of John

In the fairly recent past, it was assumed that Mark's Gospel, widely considered the first Gospel to be written, was to be trusted as more historically accurate than John's. John was thought to have been written very late and to be highly "theologized." This prejudice against the "historicity" of the Johannine Gospel goes back to early in the third century. Clement of Alexandria wrote: "Last of all, aware that the physical facts had been recorded in the [other] Gospels, . . . John wrote a spiritual Gospel."[20] It is now generally recognized, however, that the intention of all the gospel writers was primarily theological, Mark no less than John.[21] Moreover, as we shall see, the finding of the Dead Sea Scrolls and recent archaeological discoveries have radically altered our attitude toward the historical value of the Gospel of John. When the Gospels disagree, serious consideration must be given to the possible accuracy of the Johannine account.

WHOSE AUTHORITY?

As we search the Gospels for historical facts, we ask whose authority stands behind the divergent accounts. One reason for former confidence in the historical accuracy of the Synoptics was the belief that they had been written by apostles or disciples of apostles. That attribution, based on second-century information about the origins of the Gospels, has been seriously questioned by many modern scholars. They would suggest that the first Gospel was almost surely not written by Matthew or any other eyewitness, and that the attitude toward Peter in the second Gospel makes it highly unlikely that it was written by a disciple of Peter. As for Luke, while one commentator suggests that Luke/Acts is so distant from Pauline thought that Luke as a direct disciple of Paul is unlikely to have written it,[22] another is convinced that the arguments about the distance of Luke from Paul are not sufficient to overcome the traditional identification of the author of the Gospel and Acts with Luke, the sometime companion of Paul.[23]

As for the Gospel of John, tradition attributed authorship to John, the apostle and son of Zebedee, who would have been an eyewitness to the events in the ministry of Jesus. This attribution was accepted until the end of the last century, when extreme skepticism developed concerning the date, authorship and sources of the Johannine Gospel.

THE DATE OF JOHN
The question of the date is significant because the closer the writing of the Gospel is to the events, the more historically credible could be the account. Ancient tradition held that the Gospel of John had been written by John, the son of Zebedee, in his very old age. During the past century, however, dates have been proposed ranging from as late as 170 to as early as 65.

The date 170 for John, proposed by German scripture scholars in the last century, ruled out the possible authorship by John, the son of Zebedee, and supported an extreme skepticism concerning the Gospel as a source of reliable historical information. The Gospel was thought to be a product of the world dominated by the language,

The Credibility of John

thought and customs of Greek culture that had spread throughout the east since the time of Alexander the Great (336-323 BCE).[24] John was judged to have no historical value and was presumed to be completely out of touch with the Palestine of Jesus of Nazareth. Its few "facts," which served as the framework for the author's Hellenistic theology, were presumed to have been taken from Matthew, Mark or Luke. However, the skeptical confidence in the date 170 was destroyed with the publication in 1935 of a papyrus fragment of the Gospel (P^{52}) from early in the second century. The result of that discovery was to push a possible date for John back to around 100.

An important new development in determining dates has come with the now widespread realization that gospel accounts may reflect events and conditions in the church at the time and in the place where each Gospel originated, rather than the situation during the ministry of Jesus. This has led scholars to recognize elements in the gospel accounts that could scarcely have been present at the time of Jesus, but can quite plausibly fit into a period in the life of the community in which the Gospel was written. If details in a gospel passage do not fit in the time of Jesus, but do fit in a later period in the history of the community, then the Gospel cannot have been written earlier than that point in the community's history.

John's account of the healing of the man born blind (9:1-41) contains a good example of the introduction of a later situation in the church into the account of an event in the ministry of Jesus. His parents refused to answer questions about how

The Credibility of John

their son was healed "because they feared the Jews, for the Jews had already agreed that if any one should confess him to be Christ, he was to be *put out of the synagogue*" (9:22). Such a threat of expulsion from the synagogue is scarcely credible during the ministry of Jesus, but it may have been real enough at the time the Gospel was written.[25] The date of the writing of the Gospel could not have been earlier than a time when such a threat could have occurred.

I question a theory, widely held among contemporary scripture scholars, that this threat of being "expelled from the synagogue" reflects a situation around the year 85. According to this theory, the rabbis at Yavneh introduced a curse against the heretics, *minim*, which produced the final, radical break between the young church and the synagogue.[26] The backers of the theory contend that up until the Jewish War (66-70), there were extended periods of peaceful coexistence between the Christian Jews and their fellow Jews, despite occasional persecution by the Jewish leaders in Jerusalem. This peaceful coexistence is said to have changed after the fall of Jerusalem in 70 when the priests disappeared from history as leaders of the Jewish people and the Pharisees who became the leaders withdrew to Yavneh.

The theory proposes the following development. With the loss of the Temple and sacrifices, only the Law remained as a source of unity for the widely scattered Jewish people. In the siege mentality of the time, the rabbis at Yavneh, the successors of the Pharisees, placed great emphasis on faithfulness to the Law. Paul's insistence that Gentile converts

The Credibility of John

were not bound by the Law was well known. Moreover, according to a very early tradition, the Christian Jews had fled from Jerusalem to Pella to escape the Roman siege that ended in the destruction of Temple and city.[27] The loyalty of Christian Jews would have been suspect.

According to the theory, the rabbis at Yavneh added a curse against the heretics, the Twelfth Benediction, *birkat ha-minim*, to the Eighteen Benedictions that were recited three times daily in all synagogues. Because the Christians would be unwilling to invoke a curse upon themselves by recitation of this prayer, they would be exposed and forced to leave the synagogue. It has been proposed that the phrase "to be put out of the synagogue" (*aposynagōgos*, Jn 9:22) referred to a formal excommunication. Thus the story of the man born blind was said to have a twofold reference. It is about a blind Jew in Jerusalem healed by Jesus, but it is also about members of the Johannine community forced out of the synagogue by the "awesome Benediction" at the time the Gospel was written.[28] If it could be established that "being thrown out of the synagogue" in John refers to the curse said to have been imposed at Yavneh around 85, the Gospel of John would have had to be written after that date.

There are, however, several difficulties with this theory. There is doubt that the threefold use of *aposynagōgos* in John refers to a formal excommunication and, in addition, both date and significance of the action at Yavneh are historically problematical.

The date of the addition of the *birkat ha-minim* to

the Eighteen Benedictions is not at all certain. Moreover, actions against Christians similar to those that the theory places around 85 were already taking place several decades earlier.[29] Expulsion of Christians from the synagogues had begun with the death of Stephen (probably in 36) before the conversion of Paul. Paul's mission communities were often formed precisely because his converts had been expelled from the synagogue. The violence of these controversies can be seen from the five floggings Paul received in the course of his missionary work (2 Cor 11:24). Acts describes the severe harm Herod (Agrippa I) did to the members of the church in Jerusalem around 43 when he had James, the son of Zebedee, put to death by the sword (12:1). Later the stoning of James, the brother of the Lord, and other leading Christian Jews by the high priest Annas II in 62 may have led to the flight of the Christian Jews to Pella.[30]

If the effect of this curse in the Eighteen Benedictions was an early radical separation of church and synagogue, how can we account for the situation three centuries later in Antioch when St John Chrysostom preached his bitter, abusive attacks against the Jews in an effort to stop the many Christians in Antioch and other cities of the east from taking part in Jewish worship.[31] Is such participation by Christians in synagogue services likely if Christians were called upon to curse themselves? Indeed, no single, widely promulgated edict seems to have brought about the final, radical break between Judaism and Christianity. Rather the separation seems to have been the result of a long process that varied from place to place.[32]

The Credibility of John

The Gospel's polemical use of the phrase "the Jews" is claimed to support a date after Yavneh, since that usage is said to reflect the bitter disputes between church and synagogue after the radical separation brought about by the Twelfth Benediction. But the first use of "the Jews" in this polemical way is not in John but in Paul's reference in First Thessalonians to "the Jews, who killed both the Lord Jesus and the prophets" (2:14-15).[33]

The author of John could have known of conflicts between Jews and Christians in other areas in the church, like those reported in Paul and Acts, when he projected similar incidents back into his own account of the times of Jesus.[34] Thus, the Gospel could have been written close to Paul's lifetime.[35]

HELLENISTIC THOUGHT

What of the contention that the background of the Gospel is Hellenistic, without any contact with the Palestine of Jesus of Nazareth? As late as the 1960s many reputable scholars continued to hold such a point of view. Since then, however, this position has been radically undermined by a series of archaeological, documentary and textual discoveries. These findings have led other scholars "to challenge intelligently the critical views that had almost become orthodox and recognize how fragile was the base which supported the highly skeptical analysis of John. Consequently, since the Second World War there has emerged . . . a 'new look' in Johannine studies — a new look that shares much with the look once traditional in Christianity."[36]

The discovery of the Dead Sea Scrolls in 1947 effectively shattered the widely held conviction that

The Credibility of John

27

Johannine thought patterns were entirely Hellenistic
and therefore out of contact with the Palestine of
Jesus. The Scrolls, which contain the library of a
Jewish community, probably the Essenes, whose
existence spanned the years from about 140 BCE to
68 CE, give evidence of an authentic Palestinian
source of language and modes of thought that the
Johannine Gospel attributes to Jesus. Even if it
could be proved that Jesus himself never spoke that
way, the evangelist would have expressed Jesus'
teaching in thought patterns and a vocabulary
already available in a completely Palestinian
environment.[37] Indeed, the Greek language may
have been used at every level of society in
Jerusalem and Galilee. About forty percent of all
epitaphs unearthed in the Jerusalem area are in
Greek.[38] "Contemporary research favours a
Palestinian, Old Testament, Jewish setting for the
thought of the Gospel."[39]

DETAILS ABOUT PLACES AND PERSONS
Support for the claim that the Johannine Gospel is
often more historically credible than the Synoptics
can be found in its many more exact geographical
details about the area in which the events took
place, especially since the accuracy of its
information is often supported by recent
archaeological discoveries. Locations mentioned in
John but not in the Synoptics include: "Cana,
Tiberias, Sychar, Joseph's field, Jacob's well, Mount
Gerizim, Aenon near Salim, Bethany beyond Jordan,
the house of Mary, Martha, and Lazarus, the place
of Jesus' meeting with Martha, the tomb of Lazarus,
Ephraim, the pool of Bethesda, the pool of Siloam,

The Credibility of John

Solomon's Portico, the Wadi Kidron, the garden where Jesus was arrested, the door of the High Priest's court, the Pavement/Gabbatha, the garden in which Jesus' tomb was located."[40]

A good example of how much more specific John is than the Synoptics can be seen by comparing Luke's and John's treatment of their common tradition about Martha and Mary. Luke, who claims to have checked the sources, writes, "While they were on their way Jesus came to a village" (10:38). He gives no reason for the visit, no name of place or indication of time, except that it seems to be near the beginning of the final journey, so probably closer to Galilee than to Jerusalem.

In sharp contrast with the vagueness of Luke, John has detailed accounts of two separate visits: the first to raise Lazarus from the dead (11:1-12) and the second for the anointing (12:1-8). He tells us the name of the village, Bethany, its distance from Jerusalem (fifteen stades, just under two miles). For the second visit we learn that he came from Ephraim and that he arrived six days before passover, a precise date that we can locate on the calendar. Such detail seems to come from genuine memory. "Furthermore, recent archaeological studies have tended to reinforce the belief that in the Johannine topography we are in touch with a tradition which knew Palestine intimately."[41]

These findings have led to a significant reevaluation of the different Gospels as sources for historical information, especially on the passion narrative. D. E. Nineham, a leading commentator on Mark formerly considered the most factual of the Gospels, writes that "it is impossible, on the basis of Mark, to recover in any detail the historical facts about the Last Supper or about the trial, or trials, of Jesus."[42] C. H. Dodd has written "that behind the Fourth Gospel lies an ancient tradition, independent of the other Gospels, and meriting serious consideration as a contribution to our knowledge of the historical facts concerning Jesus Christ."[43] Schnackenburg writes that "the Johannine tradition . . . gives a not inconsiderable amount of extra information, that merits respect even from the historical point of view. This is true above all of the tradition concerning the Baptist, and the passion narrative."[44] And according to Brown, "We are not to assume facilely that the synoptic Gospels are recording the historic fact and that John has theologically reorganized the data. . . . We are coming to realize more and more that the critics have played us false in their minimal estimate of the historicity of the Fourth Gospel."[45]

THE CHRONOLOGY OF THE MINISTRY

Although none of the evangelists seem to have our contemporary concern for historical accuracy, the length of Jesus' ministry is an example of where John may be a better source for historical clues than the Synoptics. The Synoptics mention only one passover from the call of the first disciples to Jesus' trip to Jerusalem to suffer and die. Hence we might conclude from their accounts that the ministry lasted only one year and that Jesus had never previously visited Jerusalem as an adult. Yet there are all kinds of subtle hints in the Synoptics that he has been there before, not least his cry over Jerusalem: "*How often* have I longed to gather your

The Credibility of John

children, as a hen gathers her brood under her wing: but you would not" (Mt 23:37; Lk 13:34). Moreover, the supposition of a ministry extending only from one passover to another is contradicted by the synoptic story itself.[46]

In John, on the other hand, there is reference to three passovers for the first and third of which Jesus went up to Jerusalem. So the ministry would have lasted over two years. Almost all of the events in the Synoptics, except the cleansing of the Temple, the final meeting of the Jewish great council to plot Jesus' death, the date of the passover, and the agony in the garden, can be easily fitted into the Johannine time-frame.[47] For the cleansing of the Temple, of course, the Synoptics with only one trip to Jerusalem had no choice but to place the event at the end.

The Synoptics probably did not intend to suggest that the ministry lasted only one year. They simply do not supply the information we need to develop a credible chronology. The Gospel of John does.

THE BELOVED DISCIPLE

From where does the Gospel of John get its detailed, often reliable, historical information? The Gospel itself claims to base its authority on the eyewitness account of the Beloved Disciple, "This is the disciple who is bearing witness to these things, and who has written these things; we know that his testimony is true" (21:24). Moreover, for the events immediately following the death of Jesus, the writer affirms, "He who saw it has borne witness — his testimony is true, and he knows that he tells the truth — that you also may believe" (19:35). No other Gospel makes such claims.

There is now widespread agreement that the Beloved Disciple was a real person. To claim that he is only an ideal or fictional figure would imply that the author of John 21:20-23 was either deceived or deceptive when he reported distress in the community over his death.[48]

It seems likely that the Beloved Disciple was a follower of the Baptist who left him to follow Jesus. Indeed, he may be the unnamed disciple who along with Andrew was standing with the Baptist when the Baptist first pointed out Jesus as "the Lamb of God" (Jn 1:35-40). If so, he would have been one of the first to follow Jesus and thus would have been with Jesus throughout the ministry.[49] This would help explain the historical accuracy of the Gospel's account of John the Baptist.[50] The Beloved Disciple's presence at the Last Supper establishes him as a credible witness for the final events in Jerusalem. As the hero of the community in which it was written, he would have been their principal source of information for the events described in their Gospel. Hence the opinion "that there is one dominant creative authority and teacher behind the Johannine corpus" becomes highly plausible.[51]

Traditionally, the Beloved Disciple has been identified with the apostle John, brother of James and son of Zebedee. There is now widespread disagreement among scholars about that identification. Brown[52] and Schnackenburg[53] originally accepted the identification of the Beloved Disciple with the son of Zebedee. Although both have more recently rejected that identification, they nevertheless suggest that we have an account

The Credibility of John

stemming from a disciple who was present at the events, not, however, one of the Twelve.[54]

Among the reasons advanced for rejecting the identification of John, the son of Zebedee, as the Beloved Disciple and as the source behind the Gospel is the contention that the language and the development of christology and realized eschatology of the Gospel are all beyond the capabilities of a relatively poor and uneducated Galilean fisherman.

The presumption of poverty is certainly not supported by what we know of John from the other Gospels. His father's household included hired servants (Mk 1:20) and his mother Salome was one of the women who ministered to Jesus (Mk 15:40) and as Luke suggests did so "out of their means" (8:3). The household seems to resemble that of the father of the Prodigal Son in the parable, or perhaps, Joseph of Arimathea.

As for language, it has been suggested that the Gospel is written in "good, if unambitious, Greek with an Aramaic accent" — just what could be expected of a Galilean who lived across the Sea of Galilee from the Greek-speaking Decapolis and who was well enough known to the high priest in Jerusalem to get Peter past the portress into the courtyard of the high priest's residence (Jn 18:16). If the Beloved Disciple was a follower of the Baptist, who may very plausibly have had contacts with the Essenes, there is no reason why he could not have recast his account of the teaching of Jesus in the language and thought patterns that could have come from association with that community. As we questioned earlier, is it firmly established that Jesus himself never used such language?

The Credibility of John

As for the development of christology and realized eschatology, how likely is it that the name of the overtowering genius of the first century responsible for that significant writing has unfortunately been lost? More plausible is the explanation that this development occurred in the prayers, teaching and preaching of the beloved follower whom the Gospel of John suggests was with Jesus throughout his ministry, and whom the Synoptics and Acts place at the center of that ministry and of the important years of development in the early church. Of him the Gospel affirms, "This is the disciple who is bearing witness to these things, and has written these things; and we know that his testimony is true" (21:24).

An interesting fact about this Gospel is its more frequent use than the Synoptics of significant names: Philip twelve times and Thomas seven, against only once each in the Synoptics. Andrew is mentioned six times in John against four in Mark and two in Matthew.[55] By way of contrast, how do we explain the failure of this Gospel to mention by name James as well as John, the sons of Zebedee, both so prominent in the Synoptics and Acts and referred to only once in John 21 and then not by name but only as "the sons of Zebedee"? Does not reticence to speak of his own family, rather than ignorance, seem to be the plausible explanation for this glaring omission? But, you will say, there isn't anything very modest about calling yourself "the Beloved Disciple." I suggest that this was the title given him in the Johannine community and that the last editor inserted it, not consistently, but in some key places in the final version of the Gospel.

The Credibility of John

Robinson is convinced "that the man behind John's Gospel, the Beloved Disciple, is indeed the son of Zebedee, as tradition has unanimously asserted."[56]

The problem of identity is not critical for the question of the historical reliability of John. Nor is it essential that the Gospel have been written by one of the Twelve. What is important is the increased recognition of the presence of an eyewitness as the source behind this Gospel. When the Gospels do not seem to be in accord, I propose that we take the evidence of the Johannine Gospel seriously.

The Passion

In the passion narrative we face the key issue for understanding the impact of the Gospels on the growth of anti-Semitism in Christian Europe: who had the major responsibility for the death of Jesus, the Jews or the Romans? There are contradictions in the evidence. Paul wrote around the year 51 that Jesus was killed by the Jews (1 Th 2:15) and about three years later in Galatians 3:1 that he was crucified. Crucifixion, however, was unknown to Jewish law and practice, but was the punishment used by the Romans for non-citizens. Tacitus admits (or claims) responsibility for the Romans,[57] and the tractate *Sanhedrin* in the Babylonian Talmud claims it for the Jews.[58] So the possibility of involvement of both parties must be considered.[59]

The classical Christian position, taught and preached for centuries and influential as a source of anti-Semitism, has been that the Jewish leaders were the prime initiators and movers in the arrest, trial and sentencing. The leaders did not believe that Jesus was the Messiah and considered him a threat to themselves and to the nation. They arrested him, tried him on charges of blasphemy, and sentenced him to death. Lacking the power to execute anyone under the Roman occupation, or wanting to shift responsibility for his death on the Romans, they brought Jesus before Pilate on trumped-up political charges, persuaded the people to call for his crucifixion, and blackmailed Pilate into carrying out their will.[60]

At the other extreme is the position of those who deny that the Jewish authorities were involved in any way, even as tools of the Romans. In between

The Passion

these two extremes are two positions. There are those who would insist that the Jewish leaders were deeply involved but that the main legalities were carried out by the Romans.[61] Others considered the Romans the prime movers who, convinced that Jesus was a troublemaker, forced cooperation from a compliant Jewish leadership.

There is a widely held modern position that there was willing collaboration between the Roman procurator and the Jerusalem leadership under Caiaphas. In *Jewish Antiquities* (18:34-35) Josephus shows the high level of Roman control over the high priestly office. Valerius Gratus, procurator from 15 to 26, upon entering office had deposed the high priest Annas and within a three year period had appointed and deposed three other high priests. In Caiaphas, the son-in-law of Annas, he finally found one who served satisfactorily under him for eight years. Caiaphas continued in office for another ten years during the procuratorship of Pontius Pilate.[62] When Pilate was removed from office, his successor Vitellius immediately deposed Caiaphas "who was likely to be unpopular as a tool of Pilate."[63] John's mention of Roman soldiers in the arrest supports a theory of collusion.

Since, as we shall see, John's passion narrative gives evidence of much more limited Jewish responsibility than do Mark's and Matthew's, it becomes important to determine which of these divergent accounts is more historically plausible. Realization that John's account is more historically credible than Mark's and Matthew's might have lessened Mark's and Matthew's influence as sources for anti-Semitism in the past and might help

The Passion

prevent Christian anti-Semitism in the future.

We will begin our analysis of the gospel accounts with their different timing of the final meeting of the Sanhedrin to plot Jesus' death and then work through to the end of the passion narrative. Some of their disagreements about what happened are not significant for determining responsibility for Jesus' death, but even these can help us decide which account is more plausible when they disagree, John or Mark and Matthew.

THE SANHEDRIN MEETS TO CONDEMN

The Sanhedrin at this time was composed of "the chief priests and elders and scribes" (Mk 14:43). The chief priests and elders would have been Sadducees, members of the powerful lay and priestly families in Jerusalem. Some of the scribes would have been Pharisees, whose power in the Sanhedrin was limited. Historically, "it seems reasonable to limit Jewish involvement to the upper class, the powerful Jerusalem lay and priestly families."[64] The Pharisees are not mentioned in the passion narrative in any of the Gospels.

Mark, followed by Matthew, places the decisive meeting two days before the passover: "It was now two days before the passover and the feast of Unleavened Bread. And the chief priests and the scribes were seeking how to arrest him by stealth, and kill him; for they said 'Not during the feast lest there be a tumult of the people'" (Mk 14:1-2; Mt 26:2-3). However, the betrayal of Jesus by Judas precipitated the arrest. Luke says only that when "the feast of Unleavened Bread drew near . . . the chief priests and scribes were seeking how to put

The Passion

38

him to death" (22:1).

The account in John places the meeting of the
Sanhedrin several weeks before passover,
immediately after the report to the Pharisees of the
raising of Lazarus from the grave. "So the chief
priests and the Pharisees gathered the council, and
said, 'What are we to do? For this man performs
many signs. If we let him go on thus, everyone
will believe in him, and the Romans will come and
destroy both our holy place and our nation.' But
one of them, Caiaphas, who was high priest that
year, said to them, 'You know nothing at all; you
do not understand that it is expedient for you that
one man should die for the people, and that the
whole nation should not perish'" (Jn 11:47-50).

Some scholars think that this meeting in John was
a plenary session of all of the members of the
Sanhedrin, with a formal trial *in absentia*.[65] Yet
John's account scarcely supports that interpretation.
Both the casual way in which Caiaphas is
introduced and the bluntness of his words to those
present, suggest that this was more like a strategy
meeting with sympathetic associates than a formal
session of the entire Sanhedrin at which Caiaphas
was presiding. It certainly has none of the
characteristics of a formal trial such as we find in
Mark's and Matthew's report of a night trial after
the arrest.[66]

Who would have been invited to this informal
meeting of the Sanhedrin and would therefore have
been responsible for the decision that Jesus should
die? We know from both Luke and John that Jesus
had sympathizers in the council. Luke tells us that
Joseph of Arimathea "was a member of the council,

The Passion

a good and righteous man, who had not consented to their purpose and deed" (23:50-51) and John reports that Nicodemus was also a member of the council who at an earlier meeting of that body had been rebuffed when he called for a fair hearing for Jesus (7:50-52). John also informs us later in the Gospel that "many even of the authorities believed in him, but for fear of the Pharisees did not confess it" (12:42). It seems likely that only members of the council who were known to be hostile to Jesus would have been present and therefore responsible for the decision to seek his death. So when Mark reports that "the whole council held a consultation" (15:1) and Matthew writes that "all the chief priests and elders took counsel against Jesus to put him to death" (27:1), we seem to have a broad generalization that needs to be narrowed down.

Whoever was there, information about the decision was leaked, for when Jesus learned of their plan, he withdrew with his disciples to a town named Ephraim in the country near the wilderness. We do not know how long he stayed there, so we cannot pin down the length of time between the council meeting and his arrest. But we know that six days before the passover he came to Bethany to the home of Martha, Mary and Lazarus, where he was anointed (11:47--12:11). The following day as he came into Jerusalem he was met by "a great crowd" with palm branches and song (12:12-13).

When compared with the Synoptics, the detailed information about this sequence of events in John, with names, times and places, suggests that it could well be the report of a participant.

The Passion

THE LAST SUPPER[67]

The Synoptics state that the Last Supper was a passover meal, "And *on* the first day of Unleavened Bread, when they sacrificed the passover lamb, his disciples said to him, 'Where will you have us go and prepare for you to eat the passover?'" (Mk 14:12). By putting the sacrifice of the lambs "*on* the first day of Unleavened Bread," instead of *before* the first day, Mark has reversed the proper order of the events as they would have been understood by any ordinary Jew of the time.[68] Is this a small sign that Mark is not always too reliable with the historical facts? Matthew corrects Mark's error.

John, however, says that the Supper took place "before the feast of the passover" (13:1). Moreover, on the morning after the Supper, when Jesus was taken before Pilate, the passover had not yet begun, as the chief priests "did not enter the praetorium, so that they might not be defiled, but might eat the passover" that night (18:28). Again, twice after the death of Jesus John tells us that it was still the "day of Preparation" (19:31, 40) and that the bodies could not remain on the cross as the approaching sabbath was "a high day," that is, the first day of an important feast (19:31).[69]

So the witness of the Fourth Gospel is that the passover that year began on Friday evening and that the Last Supper took place on the night before. The Last Supper, therefore, would have been a final fellowship meal and not a passover meal.[70] John's chronology is much more plausible than that of the Synoptics. The level of activity on that Friday — trials, flogging, carrying of a cross, Simon of Cyrene coming in from the fields, crucifixion, purchase of

The Passion

spices, a tomb opened and a burial — is not likely to have taken place on the first day of the feast that celebrated Israel's liberation from Egyptian bondage. With the tensions under Roman rule, such an action could easily have led to a riot.

IN THE GARDEN OF GETHSEMANE

In the synoptic account, Jesus and his disciples went from the supper room to Gethsemane where Jesus suffered the experience called "the agony in the garden." John has the visit to the garden, but no agony. There are, however, impressive parallels between the synoptic account of the agony and Jesus' announcement of the hour of his glorification earlier in John, when some of the Greeks asked Philip if they could see Jesus (12:23, 27-28):

John	Mark
"The hour has come for the Son of man to be glorified" (12:23).	"The hour has come" (14:41).
"Now my soul is troubled" (12:27).	"My soul is very sorrowful" (14:34).
"Father, save me from this hour" (12:27).	"He fell on the ground and prayed that if it were possible, the hour might pass him by . . . 'Abba, Father . . . remove this cup from me'" (14:35-36).

The Passion

And finally, a last although weaker parallel, the voice from heaven that the people mistook for an angel in John (12:29) resembles Luke's reference to the appearance of an angel from heaven to strengthen Jesus in his agony (22:43).

It is unlikely that the primitive church would invent such an incident about its glorified Lord, but the account in all the Synoptics makes it clear that the only possible witnesses were asleep. It would be quite characteristic of gospel writing for the synoptic authors to flesh out their limited account with suitable material found elsewhere in the tradition. They have created for their own readers who face trials and persecution a model of prayer closely related to the Lord's Prayer.

John's location of the Gethsemane material somewhat earlier and in a different situation from that of the Synoptics may well be more historically accurate.[71] Later we will see, in their account of a night trial before the Sanhedrin, a similar case where John has more plausibly located at an earlier date materials that Mark and Matthew may have gathered together to create a single event.

THE ARREST

All the Gospels agree on the concern of the leaders for Jesus' popularity with the people, but only in John is a political motive made clear: the fear that his popularity could lead to an uprising which would provoke Roman reaction and lead to the destruction of the holy place and nation. The Gospels agree that the arrest was precipitated by the treachery of Judas.

The Passion

A significant divergence occurs, however, in the accounts of the arrest. Initially, all of the Synoptics speak of the presence of "a crowd." Mark writes of "a crowd . . . from the chief priests and the scribes and the elders" (14:43). In Matthew it is "a great crowd . . . and the elders of the people" (26:47). At first Luke also speaks of a crowd, but then specifies that those whom Jesus addresses are "the chief priests and captains of the Temple and the elders" (22:52). The elders have been identified as wealthy nobles. (We may recall that the Pharisees are not mentioned as present in any Gospel after John 11:57.) Has Luke, in verse 52, given us a description of the complete makeup of the crowd, priests, temple guards and elders with no involvement of the people, so that his story is somewhat closer to what we find in John? For in the Fourth Gospel no crowd of people is mentioned in the account of the arrest.

However, in John's account of the arrest, there are Roman soldiers under the command of a Roman officer in addition to temple officers. John writes that Judas led "a band of soldiers (*speiran*, literally, the cohort) and some officers from the chief priests and the Pharisees" (18:3). "Cohort" definitely refers to Roman soldiers, either the cohort of 600 men or the maniple of 200.[72] The participation of Roman soldiers in the arrest is confirmed later in John, "So the band of soldiers and their captain (*chiliarchos*, literally tribune) and the officers of the Jews seized Jesus and bound him" (18:12). Not only does the word for "captain" refer to an officer in the Roman army, but the cohort and tribune are clearly distinguished from the Jewish officers involved in

The Passion

the arrest.

In his Dublin lectures Brown suggests that this picture of early Roman involvement "could be extraordinarily important because it would be impossible that Roman soldiers and a centurion marched without Pilate's permission."[73] Moreover, in his commentary Brown observed, "It is not easy to write off a picture of Roman involvement in Jesus' arrest as the evangelist's invention. . . ." Where John disagrees with the Synoptics about what happened in the garden, the agony, and who conducted the arrest, his "information or approach has considerable plausibility as representing older tradition."[74]

A TRIAL AT NIGHT?

The account of a night trial of Jesus before the Sanhedrin, mentioned only in Mark and Matthew, has long been an important source of evidence for Jewish culpability. It supported the contention that the real Jewish charge against Jesus was the religious charge that he deserved to die for blasphemy, that is, his claim to be the Son of God. Before Pilate, however, the leaders falsely changed the charge into the political accusation that Jesus claimed to be a king in opposition to Caesar.

Mark and Matthew describe a formal night trial with witnesses before the whole Sanhedrin, presided over by Caiaphas the high priest (Mk 14:53; Mt 26:57). After a sentence of death for blasphemy, "some [members of the council] began to spit on him and to cover his face, and to strike him, saying to him 'Prophesy!' And the guards received him with blows" (Mk 14:65; Mt 26:66-67).

The Passion

After reporting Peter's denials, the evangelists describe the end of the trial with its decision to deliver Jesus to Pilate (Mk 15:1; Mt 27:1-2).

We do not have information on the law governing Jewish trials at the time of Jesus. But if the legal norms found later in the Mishnah applied, this trial would have been sufficiently irregular to cast doubt on the historicity of the account.[75]

Luke, with Mark before him, has shifted the time to morning and significantly changed the hearing's character. It is much less structured and there is no clear charge of blasphemy or a sentence. In fact, it gives the impression of having been a preliminary interrogation, preparatory to taking Jesus before Pilate.

What Luke writes is not unlike what we find in John's description of a night appearance before Annas, the father-in-law of Caiaphas (18:13-24). This hearing, without witnesses or a verdict, reads like the police interrogation of a newly arrested prisoner before handing him over to the proper authorities for trial.[76] So Luke and John seem to agree that there was only one trial, the trial before Pilate "and that may be close to our historical reality."[77]

We have already seen a case, the agony in the garden, where the Synoptics located in the passion narrative material that was more plausibly placed earlier in the ministry in John. Similarly, there are important elements in the synoptic account of a trial before the Sanhedrin that can be found in other contexts in John:

The Passion

The Synoptic Account	John
The decision that Jesus should die, made two days before the passover, (Mk 14:65; Mt 26:66)	was made several weeks before the passover at a meeting presided over by Caiaphas (Jn 11:47-53).
The accusation of the witness about the destruction of the temple (Mk 14:58; Mt 26:60-61)	corresponds to Jesus' statement, "Destroy this temple, and in three days I will raise it up" (Jn 2:19).
The high priest's question in Mark and Matthew, "Are you the Christ, the Son of the Blessed?" and Jesus' answer, "I am" (Mk 14:61-62; Mt 26:63-64; Lk 22:67)	is similar to John's account of the bitter argument with "the Jews" on the previous feast of the Dedication (10:24-25, 33, 36).
Luke at the morning hearing, "'If you are the Christ, tell us.' But he said to them, 'If I tell you, you will not believe; and if I ask you, you will not answer'" (27:67)	is close to the exchange at the feast of Dedication, "'If you are the Christ, tell us plainly.' Jesus answered them, 'I have told you, and you do not believe'" (10:24-25).
"You will see the Son of man sitting at the right hand of the power" (Mk 14:62; Mt 26:64)	is like the promise to Nathaniel of a future vision of the Son of man (Jn 1:51).

The Passion

Has Mark with a tradition of a night hearing (the one before Annas?), but no knowledge of precisely what happened, used material scattered in his sources to construct a trial that "has the air of being a summary and a synthesis of oft-repeated charges"?[78] Matthew then followed Mark's lead, while Luke's changes in the time and character of the trial before the Sanhedrin suggest his doubt about the reliability of Mark's account. Has John in the preliminary hearing before Annas given us the only "Jewish trial" that actually took place?

THE TRIAL BEFORE PILATE

All of the accounts of the trial before Pilate emphasize the political charges. In the classical account of the passion, based on Matthew and Mark, with its emphasis on Jewish responsibility, there seem to have been significantly different charges before the Sanhedrin and before Pilate. The Johannine account, however, reveals no evidence that the Jewish authorities ever charged Jesus with blasphemy. At the gathering of council members at which the decision was made to seek Jesus' death, the only concern was that Jesus' popularity could lead to an insurrection that would provoke drastic Roman reprisals. The hearing before Annas involved only questions about his teaching and followers.

The issue is political throughout the trial before Pilate. The frequent use of title "king" (*basileus*), shows that the question of kingship is being taken very seriously. Within the empire there could be only one king. In the Johannine account, after Pilate assures himself that Jesus' religious claim of

The Passion

kingship is not in conflict with imperial prerogatives, he seeks to acquit him. A despot as callous as Pilate was most unlikely to be concerned about rendering justice to a despised colonial. Perhaps he preferred releasing a harmless religious teacher like Jesus to freeing Barabbas whom Luke described as an insurrectionist and murderer (23:19) and John, as a brigand (18:40).[79] The priests, however, bent on obtaining the death penalty, insisted on the political interpretation of the word "king" and said, "If you release this man, you are not Caesar's friend; everyone who makes himself a king sets himself against Caesar" (Jn 19:12).

All four gospel accounts implicate Jerusalem leaders in the action against Jesus. What of the involvement of the people? Did the fickle crowds turn against their hero? Or do divergent accounts in the Gospels point to another possibility? Mark and Matthew are conscious of the problem. To explain why the "crowd" turned against Jesus, they report that the chief priests stirred up the crowd (Mk 15:11; Mt 27:20). According to Matthew, "all the people" called the blood curse down on themselves and on their children (Mt 27:25). In Luke, however, the people's presence with the chief priests need not mean that they agreed with the priests' accusations. But in the end, after Jesus is brought back from Herod, "the people" (*laos*, 23:13) in Luke seemed finally to have been caught up by mob psychology and called for Jesus to be crucified. We recall that Luke, in addition to using Mark, probably had also a more primitive source. Has Luke, in his sole adverse reference to "the people" in his entire passion narrative, left his more primitive source to follow Mark?[80]

John never mentions "the people" (*laos*) or "a crowd" (*ochlos*). At the end of his hearing "Annas then sent him bound to Caiaphas" (18:24). After three verses describing the third denial of Peter, the account continues with no hint of any hearing before the Sanhedrin, "Then *they* led Jesus from the house of Caiaphas to the praetorium. . . . *They* themselves did not enter the praetorium, so that *they* might not be defiled, but might eat the passover" (18:28).

WHO ARE "THEY"?

Throughout the account of the trial before Pilate "they" are usually called "the Jews" (*hoi Ioudaioi,* literally "the Judeans"). This is a generalization in the Gospel of John that covers many different categories, from the friendly Judeans who went down from Jerusalem to Bethany to console Martha and Mary over the death of their brother Lazarus to the hostile Jerusalem leaders who plotted Jesus' death. Raymond Brown contends that when John uses "the Jews" polemically, it is "almost a technical title for *the religious authorities, particularly those in Jerusalem, who are hostile to Jesus*" (emphasis in original).[81]

At two critical points of the trial, however, the generalization "the Jews" is particularized and we find out which "Jews" were actually present before Pilate and actively involved in the effort to have Jesus crucified. When "*they* cried out, 'Crucify him, crucify him,'" "they" are clearly identified as "the chief priests and the officers" (Jn 19:6). If as seems very unlikely, there were present others than the

The Passion

chief priests and officers, then like the bystanders in Luke's account of the crucifixion, they were only watchers. As Schnackenburg points out: "in John it is 'the chief priests and the officers' who raise the double cry. . . . a historically worthwhile reminder breaks through here, that those connected with the chief priests were solely responsible for the pressure put on Pilate (cf. also on 11:49ff and 18:3). This realization could have prevented much injustice against the Jewish people."[82] Notice also that in 19:15, "We have no king but Caesar," it is only the chief priests who speak.

There is no evidence in John's account of the trial before Pilate of the presence of a crowd of the people, as there clearly is in the Synoptics. The failure to recognize a generalization in John's use of the phrase "the Jews" has led more than one otherwise perceptive writer incorrectly to include a crowd of the Jewish people among the participants in the Johannine account of that trial.[83] Moreover, as Brown writes, "John's account of the trial is the most consistent and intelligible we have."[84]

If we assume that the account of the Jerusalem leaders' involvement is accurate, mixed motives have been suggested for their action. Some would have acted selfishly to protect their vested interest in the status quo. Others would have been sincerely convinced that their own interests coincided with the spiritual and temporal good of the nation. Still others, while despising the Romans, would have acted from righteous indignation against one who struck out against the Temple of God and who in speech and action subverted sacred religious customs. Brown writes,

The Passion

"There is scarcely a Christian church that cannot find in its history condemnation of good men leveled by religious assemblies with a similar variety of motives."[85]

Nostra Aetate, no. 4 of Vatican II reads:

> True, authorities of the Jews and those who followed their lead pressed for the death of Christ; still, what happened in His passion cannot be blamed upon all the Jews then living, without distinction, nor upon the Jews of today. Although the Church is the new people of God, the Jews should not be presented as repudiated or cursed by God, as if such views followed from the Holy Scriptures. All should take pains, then, lest in catechetical instruction or in preaching of God's Word they teach anything out of harmony with the truth of the Gospel and the spirit of Christ.

In view of the widespread tendency to generalize on who is to blame, it is worth emphasizing that in the Johannine account, "authorities of the Jews and those who followed their lead" does not include even the entire membership of the council, much less the people of Jerusalem.

THE CRUCIFIXION

The mocking of Jesus as he hung on the cross was another basis for the imposition of guilt on the Jewish people. In Matthew's account, Jesus was taunted by the passersby, the chief priests, the scribes and elders, as well as by the two robbers crucified with him (Mt 27:39-44; see Mk 15:29-32).

The Passion

Luke has a different picture. As a large crowd of people followed Jesus carrying the cross, Luke begins to separate the people from "the rulers." Notable are the women who beat their breasts and wail (23:27). As Jesus hung on the cross, Luke distinguishes between the silent crowd that stood by watching and the taunters: first "the rulers" (v. 35), then "the soldiers" (v. 36) and finally one of the criminals (v. 39). After the death of Jesus, Luke writes that "all of the multitudes who assembled to see the sight, when they saw what had taken place, returned home beating their breasts" (v. 48).

There are no mockers in the Johannine account. Brown includes the "mockeries" in a list of twenty "details of the synoptic narrative *not* found in John." Since the mockeries would have served as excellent vehicles for Johannine theology, their omission suggests that they never occurred.[86] Luke, with Mark's account before him, also leaves out taunting by the "multitude." Do Luke and John depend on an earlier tradition in which there was no mocking by the people. Could this earlier tradition used by Luke and John come from eyewitnesses? According to Mark and Matthew, the disciples had all fled. Luke, on the contrary, reports that "all his acquaintances (*pantes hoi gnōstoi*, masc.) and the women who had followed him from Galilee stood at a distance and watched these things" (Lk 23:49). John has the Beloved Disciple "standing near" (19:26).

If the information in John, generally supported by Luke, has historical value, the people in Jerusalem at the feast were not involved in the arrest, trial, or mockery of the Crucified.

The Passion

Who Were "The Jews"?

The conviction that all of the Gospels are sources for anti-Semitism, with John the worst, is deeply ingrained. Even those who can be convinced that John's passion narrative, properly interpreted, is minimally a source for anti-Semitism, still point out the anti-Semitic impact of the seventy-one times the expression "the Jews" (*hoi Ioudaioi*) is used throughout that Gospel. Need that phrase, with its centuries-old negative connotation, continue to contribute to a widespread perception that John is irremediably the most anti-Judaic of the Gospels? I think not. A careful interpretation in context of John's many uses of *hoi Ioudaioi* reveals that they also should not have supported later anti-Semitism.

"The Jews" is not an exact transliteration of the Greek *hoi Ioudaioi*. Sometimes it should be translated "Judeans."[87] A good example is John 7:1, "After this Jesus went about in Galilee; he would not go about in Judea (*Ioudaía*), because the Jews (*hoi Ioudaioi*) sought to kill him." Apparently, Jesus was safe in Galilee, but not safe in Judea. Since the inhabitants of both areas were Jews, it becomes clear that Jesus was not afraid of all Jews but only of some Jews, and they lived in Judea. So it would seem that it would be more accurate to translate *hoi Ioudaioi* as "Judeans." But wait, does the text refer to all the "Judeans"? In his commentary Brown suggests that it refers only to the Jerusalem authorities.[88] We have already quoted his statement that in polemical passages "the Jews" is almost a technical title for the hostile, religious authorities, especially those in Jerusalem.

Barnabas Lindars, a respected British scripture

scholar, also considers this a case of the more restricted sense of the phrase *hoi Ioudaioi* that refers to the Jewish authorities in Jerusalem.[89] Schnackenburg, in his highly regarded commentary, lists it among twenty-six examples where it refers to "hostile circles of unbelievers among the influential classes (Pharisees) and the responsible authorities (high priests)."[90] D. Moody Smith, a scripture scholar at Duke University, says that the phrase "refers to certain authorities rather than to the people as a whole" and that when it is misread, the phrase makes the Gospel appear anti-Semitic.[91] This inaccuracy of translation occurs in other parts of the text as well, contributing to the widespread perception that John's Gospel is anti-Semitic. If, therefore, the correct meaning of the text in so many cases in John's Gospel is the Jerusalem authorities who opposed Jesus, should not an effort be made to avoid an incorrect translation that for centuries has made the Gospel appear anti-Semitic?

The argument is usually made that such a correction would be only a paraphrase and that it is not scholarly to use several words to translate a single word in the Greek text. Yet we have already dealt with a situation in a different context in John in which widely respected translations used several words to render one word in the Greek. In the account of the man born blind, his parents "feared the Jews (*tous Ioudaious*), for the Jews (*hoi Ioudaioi*) had already agreed that if anyone should confess him to be the Christ, he was to be *put out of the synagogue (aposynagōgos)*" (Jn 9:22). If *aposynagōgos* can be translated "put out of the synagogue" in

order to capture its correct meaning, *tous Ioudaious*
and *hoi Ioudaioi* could be translated in the same
verse as "the Jerusalem officials, leaders, or
authorities." But even here further caution is
needed. Use of the definite article "the" (*tous* and
hoi) implies that all of the Jerusalem leaders were
involved. We have already seen, however, that
Nicodemus, Joseph of Arimathea, and other
believers in Jesus were members of the Sanhedrin
(Jn 3:1-2; 7:47-52; 12:42-43; 19:38-42).

In their November 1990 meeting in Washington,
the American Catholic bishops began to address the
language issue with this recommendation, "The
expression 'the Jews' in the Fourth Gospel is [to be]
translated as 'the Jewish authorities' or 'the Jewish
religious leaders' or 'the Jewish leaders' or the
'Jewish people,' etc."[92] This should be recognized
as only the first step toward achieving an accurate
rendition of the meaning of the phrase in context.

Another example of probable misinterpretation of
hoi Ioudaioi is found in John 8:30-59. This passage
contains the longest sustained account of
confrontation between Jesus and "the Jews" in John.
Let us recall the valuable insight of recent biblical
scholarship, namely, that the Gospels reveal what is
happening at two different periods of time. Often
they tell more about the community where the
Gospel was written than about events during the
ministry of Jesus.

Now for the period of time during the ministry,
hoi Ioudaioi in John 8:30-59 probably stands for the
hostile Jerusalem authorities. For the situation at
the time the Gospel was written, the dialogue
between Jesus and "the Jews" is usually thought to

Who Were "The Jews"?

reflect a bitter conflict between the Johannine church and the synagogue. I would suggest that it may rather reveal a clash between the Johannine church and other Christian communities composed of Christian Jews who were still committed to observance of the Law. They would be similar to the Christians of whom James and the elders spoke to Paul on his last trip to Jerusalem, "You see, brother, how many thousands there are among those who have believed; they are all zealous for the law, and they have been told about you that you teach all the Jews who are among the Gentiles to forsake Moses, telling them not to circumcise their children or observe the customs" (Acts 21:20-21).

The phrase "the Jews who *had*[93] believed in him" (Jn 8:31) has always been a source of difficulty. In John 8:30, Jesus' teaching has just led many to believe in him. Without a break, John 8:31 continues: "Jesus then said to the Jews who *had* believed in him, 'If you continue in my word, you are truly my disciples, and you will know the truth, and the truth will make you free.' They answered him, 'We are descendants of Abraham, and have never been in bondage to anyone. How is it that you say, "You will be made free?"'" There follows the most bitter polemical encounter between Jesus and "the Jews" in the entire Gospel. In it Jesus asserts that they want to kill him and have the devil as their father. They claim that Jesus is a Samaritan and has a demon. In the end, "They took up stones to throw at him; but Jesus hid himself, and went out of the Temple" (Jn 8:59).

Here is the problem. If on the level of the

Who Were "The Jews"?

situation at the time the Gospel was written, this passage reflects the bitter relations between the Johannine community and the synagogue, why are "the Jews" described as "Jews who had believed in him"? Attempted explanations include either that that there is a flaw in the final redaction of the Gospel which leaves it unclear that verses 30 and 31 refer to two different groups of people,[94] or that they were believers with weak faith who later fell away.[95]

Readers, however, in the Greek-speaking church in the first century probably understood that the reference to Jews who believed in Jesus was to believing Christians of Jewish origin.[96] In Acts and Galatians they can be recognized as those Christian Jews who insisted against Peter and Paul that Gentile converts to the church had to be circumcised and follow the Law. For the church where the Gospel was written, this passage would reflect not a conflict between the young church and the synagogue, but a struggle between two groups of believing Christians, similar to the fight Paul conducted in his letter to the Galatians against the Christian teachers who came from James in Jerusalem.

What of the objection of some scholars that the polemics in this Johannine passage are too bitter for a conflict between two groups of Christians? The bitterness in John 8 is like that of Paul who anathematizes his opponents in Galatians 1:6-9 and can say, in reference to those Christian teachers who insist on circumcision, "I wish those who unsettle you would mutilate themselves!" (5:12). It can also be compared with the attitude of the

Who Were "The Jews"?

author of First and Second John who attacks former members of his own community as demonic antichrists, false prophets, and liars (1 Jn 2:18-22; 4:1-6; 2 Jn 7) who should not be received into the house or given any greeting (2 Jn 10). First and Second John and Paul both reflect conflicts within the church and not with outsiders. Antagonism between two believing groups in the church is the plausible explanation for the conflict between Jesus and *the Jews who believed in him*" in John 8:31.[97] It is also a possible explanation of other polemical confrontations between Jesus and "the Jews" in the Gospel of John (5:16-47; 6:41, 52; 10:22-40).

Eugene LaVerdiere proposes an analysis of Luke that supports this interpretation. He suggests that the conflict in Luke between Jesus and the Pharisees represents, not a struggle between Jesus and the Pharisees, but a conflict between "neo-Pharisees" and Gentile converts in the church where the Gospel was written. LaVerdiere writes, "Many elements in Luke's narrative are incomprehensible unless we view the Pharisees as Christians."[98]

Epilogue

For almost two thousand years, a virulent anti-Semitism in Christian Europe has been fed by an account of the passion based almost entirely on Mark and Matthew — an account that placed most of the responsibility for the crucifixion on the Jewish people and their leaders who were accused of having manipulated a pliant Pontius Pilate into carrying out their purpose.

In Mark and Matthew a large crowd of Jews was involved in the arrest of Jesus. This was followed by a highly irregular night trial before the Jewish great council — with false witnesses, a condemnation to death for blasphemy and gross mockery by the leaders themselves. Before Pilate, who apparently had not been previously involved in the case, the leaders persuaded the people to cry out for his crucifixion. Most damning for future generations of Jews is Matthew's account where the people accepted full responsibility calling down Jesus' blood upon themselves and their descendants. As Jesus hung upon the cross, he was mocked by both priests and people.

In contrast, the entire Johannine account of the passion from the arrest to the burial contains not a single reference to participation by the "people" or of any presence of a "crowd." Collusion between Pilate and Caiaphas is suggested by the presence of Roman soldiers under an officer at the arrest of Jesus. There is no reference in John to any trial before the Jewish great council, but only to a preliminary hearing before Annas, the father-in-law of the high priest Caiaphas. In that hearing Jesus was questioned about his followers and his

Epilogue

teaching. In the trial before Pilate only the chief priests and temple guards seem to have been present, for none but they cried out for Jesus to be crucified. No mockery by anyone is reported while Jesus hung upon the cross. The passion narrative in John is minimally anti-Jewish. It ascribes Jewish responsibility only to hostile elements in the Jerusalem leadership.

Moreover, the same lack of anti-Jewish bias can be asserted of the rest of the Johannine Gospel. The tendency in the past to fuel anti-Semitism by that Gospel's frequent use of the phrase "the Jews," in the situations of antagonism between Jesus and the Jerusalem leadership would be eliminated by the translation of *hoi Ioudaioi* as "hostile Jerusalem leaders," where that translation is justified in the context. Several recently published translations which seek to eliminate exclusive language, for example, NAB, NRSV, NEB, NJB, did not at the same time correct "anti-Jewish" language. Such corrections should be made in lectionaries and all materials used for public reading and study, while we wait for new translations of the bible.

In view of the contradictory evidence among the Gospel accounts on the issue of responsibility and the growing respect for the historical reliability of John, what else can be done? In preaching, in seminary classes, bible schools, adult enrichment programs, and study groups, emphasis should be placed on the plausibility of the Johannine account in order to counteract the influence in past centuries of inflammatory teaching based on the almost exclusive use of Mark and Matthew in teaching and preaching.

Epilogue

All passion plays and all dramas using the passion narratives should be based primarily on John and Luke, rather than almost exclusively on Mark and Matthew as has been done in the past. Franco Zefferelli's movie made for television "Jesus of Nazareth" is a beautiful and powerful example of how the story can be told without the inflammatory material from Mark and Matthew that has been used through the centuries.

In the liturgy, however, there is a different problem especially in those churches where the long passion accounts are read with little time to preach on more plausible interpretations of the text. I propose that we address this difficulty by the way in which we schedule the reading of the passions in our church services. We should read John on the days when the congregations are largest; Mark and Matthew, when they are smallest. In most churches, Passion/Palm Sunday is the occasion on which the largest number of people hear a reading of the passion. This would probably be true of all Christian churches, but especially of Roman Catholic churches where the passion is read at several Masses on Saturday evening and Sunday, but at only one service on Good Friday. The custom of reading Matthew, Mark and Luke on a three-year cycle on Palm Sunday is less than twenty-five years old. For many centuries the passion readings from the four Gospels were fixed for certain days — Matthew on Palm Sunday, Mark on Monday, Luke on Tuesday, and John on Good Friday. Indeed, the tradition of reading Matthew, long believed to be the first Gospel written, on the first Sunday of Holy Week goes back at least to St Augustine and

Epilogue

perhaps to St Ambrose. This fact may help explain centuries of anti-Semitic preaching.

I propose that we return, with a major modification, to a fixed schedule as in previous centuries. John, which is the least anti-Jewish of the accounts and perhaps the most historically plausible would be read every year on Palm Sunday, when the largest number of hearers is present. For churches like the Roman Catholic that have services during Holy Week, Mark would always be read on Monday followed by Matthew, a source of so much anti-Semitism, on Tuesday. Luke, the least anti-Jewish of the synoptic passion narratives, would always be read on Good Friday. Its message from the cross, "Father, forgive them; for they know not what they do" (Lk 23:34) applies to the original perpetrators of the crucifixion and to us.

Epilogue

NOTES

1   "Anti-Semitism in the New Testament: The Witness of the Beloved Disciple," *Worship* 62 (September 1989) 386-401.

2   London: SCM Press Ltd 1976.

3   Oak Park, IL: Meyer-Stone 1987.

4   Jules Issac, *The Teaching of Contempt: Christian Roots of Anti-Semitism,* tr. Helen Weaver, biographical introduction by Claire Huchet Bishop (New York: Holt, Rinehart and Winston 1964).

5   Edward H. Flannery, *The Anguish of the Jews: Twenty-Three Centuries of Antisemitism,* new revised edition (New York: Paulist Press 1985) 7-27; John G. Gager, *The Origin of Anti-Semitism: Attitudes Toward Judaism in Pagan and Christian Antiquity* (New York: Oxford University Press 1983).

6   *De Oratione* 14; *Corpus Christianorum, Series Latina (CCSL)* 1:265.

7   *Adversus Iudaeos* 8:18; CCSL 2:1363-64.

8   *Series Commentariorum in Matthaeum* 124; *Patrologia Graeca* (PG) 13:1774-75.

9   Eusebius Pamphili (Bishop of Caesarea in Palestine), *Commentary on Isaiah* 1:13-15; PG 24:95B-96B.

10   *Traité des Mystères, Sources Chrétiennes* (Paris 1967) 19bis:88-90.

11   *Commentarius in Evangelium Matthaei* (on Mt 27:25) 4:27; *Patrologia Latina* 26:215.

12   Robert L. Wilken, *John Chrysostom and the Jews: Rhetoric and Reality in the Late 4th Century* (Berkeley: University of California Press 1983).

13   Saint John Chrysostom, *Discourse against Judaizing Christians (Adversus Judaeos),* tr. Paul W. Harkins (Washington: The Catholic University of America Press 1979) 154.

14   Wilken, *John Chrysostom and the Jews* 161-62.

15   Martin Luther, *Selected Psalms III* (St Louis: Concordia 1958) 267.

16   Martin Luther, *The Church in Society IV*, Franklin Sherman and Helmut T. Lehman, eds. (Minneapolis: Augsburg 1971) 268-69.

17   Prosper Guéranger, *The Liturgical Year: Passiontide and Holy Week*, tr. Laurence Shepherd OSB (Westminster, Maryland: The Newman Press 1949) 458, 460. *L'Année Liturgique* published 1841-66 had reached twenty editions by 1905 and had been translated into English in 1867, German in 1875 and Italian in 1884. It was last published in French 1948-52.

18   Vincent Taylor, *The Passion Narrative of St Luke: A Critical and Historical Investigation* (Cambridge: University Press 1972) ix.

19   Joseph A. Fitzmyer SJ, *The Gospel According to Luke* (Garden City: Doubleday 1981) 1459.

20   Eusebius, *The History of the Church from Christ to Constantine*, tr. G. A. Williamson (New York: Penguin 1983) 254.

21   "Today we recognize that each Gospel has a theological view. . . ." Raymond E. Brown SS, *The Gospel According to John* (Garden City: Doubleday 1966) xlix. See also Brown, *The Community of the Beloved Disciple: The Life, Loves, and Hates of an Individual Church in the New Testament Times* (New York: Paulist Press 1979) 380. The German scholar Martin Hengel calls Brown "the most significant commentator on the Johannine corpus at the present time. . . ." Martin Hengel, *The Johannine Question* (Philadelphia: Trinity Press 1989) 24.

22   Brown, *Community* 34.

23   Fitzmyer, *Luke* 51.

24   BCE, "before the common era," and CE, "in the common era."

25   Brown, *John* 380. See also Brown, *Responses to 101 Questions on the Bible* (New York: Paulist Press 1990) 114-15.

Notes

26 Its leading exponent has been J. Louis Martyn, *History and Theology in the Fourth Gospel, Revised and Enlarged* (Nashville: Abingdon 1979) 50-62. See also Brown, *John* lxxiv-lxxv and Rudolph Schnackenburg, *The Gospel of John* (New York: Seabury 1980) 2:250.

27 Eusebius, *History* 111.

28 Martyn, *History* 62.

29 Robinson, *Priority* 67-93. J. Moody Smith suggests that "Robinson is abreast of the literature and quite sharp." *Journal of Biblical Literature* 108 (Spring 1989) 157 and reports that Martyn no longer links his thesis to the establishment of the Twelfth Benediction in the 80s. In James H. Charlesworth, ed., *Jews and Christians* (New York: Crossroad 1990) 97.

30 Hengel, *Question* 115.

31 Saint John Chrysostom, *Discourse against Judaizing Christians* xxxvii-l. See Wilken, *John Chrysostom and the Jews* 67-68.

32 Reuven Kimmelman, "*Birkath ha-Minim* and the Lack of Evidence for an Anti-Christian Jewish Prayer in Late Antiquity," in E. P. Sanders, ed., *Jewish and Christian Self-Definition: Aspects of Judaism in the Graeco-Roman Period* (Philadelphia: Fortress 1981) 2:244.

33 John C. Hurd, "Paul Ahead of His Time: 1 Thess. 2:13-16," in Peter Richardson with David Granskou, eds., *Paul and the Gospels* (Ontario: Wilfred Laurier University Press 1986) 21-36, rejects Birger A. Pearson's claim that this passage is not authentic (*Harvard Theological Review* 64 [1971] 79-94.

34 As we shall see later, some of "the Jews" referred to may be Christian Jews.

35 Robinson, *Redating* 284. See Lamar Cribbs, "A Reassessment of the Date of Origin and the Destination of the Gospel of John," *Journal of Biblical Literature* 89 (1970) 54.

36 Brown, *John* xxi-xxii.

37 Brown, *John* xliii.

38 Hengel, *Question* 113.

Notes

39   Robert Kysar, *The Fourth Evangelist and His Gospel: An Examination of Contemporary Scholarship* (Minneapolis: Augsburg 1975) 144; Robinson, "The New Look on the Fourth Gospel," *Studia Evangelica* 1:338-50.

40   Robinson, *Priority* 52.

41   Ibid., 52-53.

42   D. E. Nineham, *The Gospel of St Mark* (London: Penguin Books 1976) 368.

43   C. H. Dodd, *Historical Tradition in the Fourth Gospel* (Cambridge: University Press 1963) 423.

44   Schnackenburg, *John* 1:42. Joseph A. Fitzmyer accepts much of what Robinson writes about the basic historical value of Johannine tradition. *Interpretation* 42 (1978) 312.

45   Raymond E. Brown, "Incidents That Are Units in the Synoptic Gospels but Dispersed in St John," *Catholic Biblical Quarterly* 23 (1961) 160.

46   For details see Robinson, *Priority* 126-27.

47   Ibid., 123-47; Hengel, *Question* 132.

48   "Of course an 'ideal figure' need not be totally ahistorical and mere fiction." Hengel, *Question* 78.

49   Brown, *Community* 31-33.

50   Schnackenburg, *John* 1:42.

51   Hengel, *Question* 93.

52   *John* xcvii.

53   *John* 3:100-04.

54   Brown, *Community* 32-34; Schnackenburg, *John* 3:383-85.

55   Hengel, *Question* 155 n. 102.

56   Robinson, *Priority* 99-122.

57   *Annals* 15:44.

58   Babylonian Talmud, *Sanhendrin* 43a.

59   Dodd, *Historical Tradition* 115-16.

60   Brown, *John* 792-802.

61   Fitzmyer, *Luke* 1456.

Notes

62   E. Mary Smallwood, *The Jews Under Roman Rule: From Pompey to Diocletian* (Leiden: E. J. Brill 1976) 159. The distinguished Israeli jurist Haim Cohn describes the high priests as Roman quislings who had bought their office at a great price. *The Trial and Death of Jesus* (New York: Harper & Row 1971) 21-23.

63   Smallwood, 172. See *Jewish Antiquities* 18:95.

64   Donald Goergen O P, *The Death and Resurrection of Jesus* (Wilmington: Michael Glazier 1988) 25, 29.

65   Among them John A. T. Robinson, "'His witness is true': A test of the Johannine claim," in Ernest Bammel and C. F. D. Moule, eds., *Jesus and the Politics of His Day* (New York: Cambridge University Press 1984) 466.

66   Brown, *John* 440.

67   Raymond E. Brown, "The Date of the Last Supper," *The Bible Today* 11 (1964) 727-33.

68   Nineham, *Mark* 376.

69   Dodd, *Historical Tradition* 109-12.

70   Vincent Taylor is convinced that Luke has abandoned his more primitive source to follow Mark. Taylor, *The Passion Narrative* 133. Did it also happen in the trial before Pilate?

71   Brown, *John* 470-71.

72   Ibid., 807.

73   Raymond E. Brown, *The Passion Narrative of the Gospels* (1988), 11 tapes distributed by Charismatic Renewal Services, Emmanuel, 3 Pembroke Park, Dublin.

74   Brown, *John* 816.

75   Ibid., 796-97.

76   Ibid., 834-35.

77   Brown's lecture in Dublin.

78   Brown, *John* 405. See E. P. Sanders, *Jesus and Judaism* (Philadelphia: Fortress Press 1985) 297-301.

79   Brown, *John* 847, 860.

80   However, see Taylor, *Passion Narrative* 89.

Notes

81 *John* lxxi. See also Urban C. von Wahlde, "The Johannine 'Jews': A Critical Survey," *New Testament Studies* 28 (1982) 47-49. Except in the passion account, this polemical use of "the Jews" in John may sometimes reveal antagonism between the Johannine community and other Christian Jews.

82 *John* 3:257-58.

83 Paul Winter, *On the Trial of Jesus*, 2nd edition revised and edited by T. A. Burkill and Geza Vermes (Berlin: Walter De Gruyter 1974) 82 and Urban C. von Wahlde, *The Earliest Version of John's Gospel: Recovering the Gospel of Signs* (Wilmington: Michael Glazier 1989) 140, 144.

84 Brown, *John* 861.

85 Ibid., 802.

86 Ibid., 914.

87 See von Wahlde, "The Johannine 'Jews': A Critical Survey," 35; *The Earliest Version* 120; and Malcolm Lowe, "Who Were the IOUDAIOI?" *Novum Testamentum* 18 (Leiden: E. J. Brill 1976) 120-24.

88 *John*, 306.

89 Barnabas Lindars SSF, *The Gospel of John* (London: Marshall, Morgan and Scott 1972) 282.

90 Schnackenburg, *John* 1:287.

91 In Charlesworth, *Jews and Christians* 82.

92 *Newsletter, National Conference of Catholic Bishops*, 26 (October/November 1990) 42.

93 RSV. Gerard S. Sloyan points out that the "*had*" in "had believed" in RSV, NRSV, and NEB "is not justified by the Greek (perfect active participle)." See note 97.

94 Brown, *John* 354; but see Brown, *Community* 77 n. 141.

95 Severino Pancaro, *The Law in the Fourth Gospel: The Torah and the Gospel, Moses and Jesus, Judaism and Christianity According to John* (Leiden: E. J. Brill 1975) 417.

Notes

70

96 See C. H. Dodd, *More New Testament Studies* (Grand
Rapids: Eerdmans 1968) 41-57 and Wayne A. Meeks, "'Am I a
Jew?' — Johannine Christianity and Judaism" in Jacob Neusner,
ed., *Christianity, and Judaism and Other Greco-Roman Cults*
(Leiden: E. J. Brill 1975) 183.

97 NJB. Sloyan suggests that the *"had"* in "had believed" in
RSV, NRSV, and NEB "is added by translators who do not get
the point being made and think that, arguing so vigorously
they cannot *still* believe in him."

98 Eugene LaVerdiere SSS, *Luke* (Wilmington, DE: Michael
Glazier 1988) xlvii.

Notes